Kathrin Köller
Irmela Schautz

THE BOOK OF
TIME

Translated from German by Paul Kelly

Prestel

Munich · London · New York

Contents

Time! What Is It?

Time is a bit like an invisible friend. It is always there, yet nobody has ever seen or touched it. Time cannot be tasted, smelled, or heard.

So what exactly is time? Can you feel it? Does it always pass by at the same speed? Does it have a beginning and an end? Or is it an illusion?

When you start thinking about time, all sorts of questions come up. And every answer only leads to more questions. But before you close the book on time, don't worry. It happens to everyone. People have been pulling their hair about time from the moment they started to think.

Nothing works without time. For example: How would a game of soccer work if time did not exist? You would not know that after two halves, extra time, and penalty kicks that the game was over. The same applies to other games, songs, math ... Time means there is a beginning and an end and that everything is possible in the first place. Without time, we are unable to think. Yet after all is said and done, we do not actually know what time is. At least one thing we can say about time is that it is a mystery we can't seem to crack!

This book is bursting with brainteasers about time. Maybe you will be able to solve a few of them? You will at least be given the tools to try. We will look at how people have thought about time over thousands of years. Gods and stories. Dragon, peacock, and elephant clocks, as well as a few other inventions designed to divide time into sections. And, of course, the best time travel machine in the world. So, if you're ready, let's begin!

The Philosophy of Time

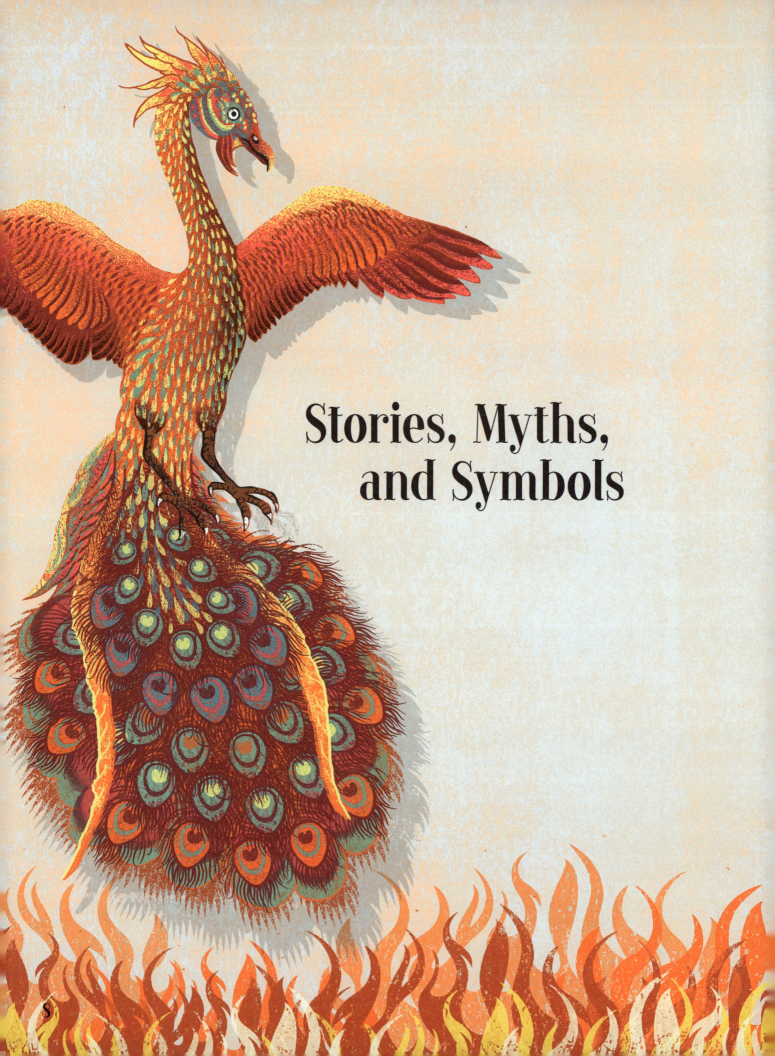

Stories, Myths, and Symbols

For as long as we can remember, people have been studying the heavens, and in doing so, gained valuable insight into time. But no one fully understood what time was, so stories were invented to explain it. And even if some of them sound fantastic and incredible, many of their heroes are still part of our lives today.

Chronos

The ancient Greeks, who lived in cities all around the Mediterranean Sea, had at least one god for every purpose. The god of time was Chronos, who had created himself out of chaos—or nothingness! Chronos was time and he was also the creator of the world. According to legend, he formed an earthly globe from which all things originated. Even now, the original Chronos with a "C" is still linked with time, as in the word "chronological." If you want to talk about something chronologically, you do it in the order that it happened. Today, how we arrange our thoughts and stories is connected to the ancient Greek god of time. Not bad, right?

Or Kronos?

Over time, Chronos was often confused with someone with a similar name—Kronos with a "K." This Kronos was a titan who had overthrown his father, Uranus, the god of the heavens. Afraid that his own children would do the same to him, Kronos gobbled them up one by one, each an important god. Just in time, their mother, Rhea, hid the youngest child, Zeus, who tricked his father into spitting the children back out. This outlandish story reveals an important aspect of the human condition, which is that Kronos gives life and also takes it away.

A raised torch signifies the morning.

A crown of rays represents the sun.

The snake symbolizes eternity.

Time to Be a Sun God

The ancient Romans, who ruled the Mediterranean after the ancient Greeks, also had a wealth of gods, many of whom they acquired from the legions of different, older cultures they conquered. The Romans gave these gods new names, new appearances, and at least one special symbol. Many Greek gods were changed into Roman ones. Even the gods of the ancient Persians, from an area we now call Iran, were transformed.

Zurvan was the Persian god of creation who personified time and space. The ancient Romans were fascinated by Zurvan. They renamed him Mithras and turned him into an invincible sun god. Mithras did well by the Romans. He was given a serpent to represent eternity and a torch to indicate the time of day, and he was crowned with a halo to signify the sun. Many centuries later, he became the role model for his "little sister," the Statue of Liberty.

Two-Faced God

One of the few gods the Romans came up with themselves was called Janus. He was the lord of time and had two heads—one looked into the past, the other could see the future. The beginning of time was especially important to Janus. At the start of religious festivities, the ancient Romans always prayed to him first. January, the first month of the year, bears his name. Nowadays, though, Janus is not held in such high regard. When we say that someone is Janus-like or Janus-faced, we mean that they are "two-faced" or, like a snake, they speak with a forked tongue.

Phoenix

The phoenix is another figure that represents time. It originates from the era of the ancient Greeks. In the US, the capital of Arizona is named after it. Sports teams, television networks, and many other organizations also bear the name of this mythical bird. According to ancient legend, after the phoenix lived for five hundred years, it set itself on fire in order to rise again from its own ashes, repeating this fantastic ritual every five hundred years.

That the phoenix can keep renewing itself gives people courage. Even today, "to rise like a phoenix" is a common phrase that suggests that even the most total failure is an opportunity to start over—regenerated, refreshed, and with renewed strength. Long live the phoenix!

Forward,
Backward,
Sideways,
Away We Go!

Yesterday was yesterday and what's gone is gone, even if we hold on to a few photos and memories of the past. The present moment is brief, immediately gone. We'll come to that later. Most of us are already thinking about tomorrow even though it's still today. We practice for the weekend basketball game or for the summer theater performance. Our mind is focused on the future because that is where time is heading—always in one direction. Just like a river. And we have no choice but to swim into the future. Well, at least that is what we believe.

Time in Circles

The ancient Egyptians experienced time differently. Past, present, and future did not exist for them. Instead, they divided time in two ways: Neheh, the time that goes around in circles, and Djet, the eternal perfection. The ancient Egyptians stumbled on to the idea that time was repetitive by watching nature. They came to realize that many things happened in cycles. The sun rises and sets again. Every year, the Nile burst its banks and flooded the land, leading to new growth. By the end of the year, there was drought. But with every new year and with every new flood, the cycle would begin again. The ancient Egyptian sun god, Ra, was responsible for this whole cycle because he appeared on the horizon every morning, sped across the skies, and then sank into the underworld of Osiris in the evening, where he united with Djet—eternity—at midnight when everything started afresh.

Round and Round

Many other cultures see time as a cycle based on the recurring patterns in nature. It is not just the sun rising and falling all the time, the moon does, too. Spring, summer, autumn, and winter occur in the same sequence. Crops grow and get harvested. This happens over and over. Is life itself a constant cycle taking place again and again? Even the ancient people of the Maya believed that the world started up anew and then perished again. The Maya believed that the jaguar, a night predator, ate the sun every evening. He would then spit out the sun in the morning.

Looking Back

So who said the future is ahead of us? The Malagasy people of Madagascar believe the future approaches us from behind and moves through us. Because we have eyes only in the front of our head, we can only "see" present and past events, while the future remains unknown because it can't be seen.

Right Here, Right Now ... So Long!

Let's forget about the past and the future for a moment. Let's look at the present—the right here and now! How long does "now" actually take? If you think about "right now," it is already over. The present is quite difficult to really catch hold of. It slips right out of your hand.

Researchers have discovered that we only feel like "now" for about 3 seconds. If something occurred longer than three seconds ago, then we regard it as already gone.

Don't Even Think about It!

Living in the present depends on how much you think about time. For example, when you are completely absorbed in a game, a book, or schoolwork, you stop thinking about everything else. At that moment, you are totally in the world of now. What's more, you are happy because you are not thinking about the past and the future.

Many adults find it hard to forget about time and live in the present. Their minds are mostly set on the future and what they have to do at a certain time. They think about what needs to be done at work, who they still need to send a message to, remembering to call grandma, when to do the shopping, and on and on and on. And to-do lists and cell phone reminders do not make things easier.

This constant life in the future is stressful and often puts grown-ups in a bad mood. It's a habit you might want to avoid. In fact, lazing about and simply not thinking about time could be good for your health! Some adults work on forgetting about time. They meditate or practice yoga and they sometimes even manage to achieve a state of timelessness.

The Long and Short of It

If you get bored or start focusing on time passing by, you find that time starts to drag. Do you think that time itself is bothered about this? For example, when you are waiting for a bus, five minutes can drag on forever. It is even worse when it comes to pain. Even though you know it will be over in five minutes, those five minutes can feel like a lifetime.

It would be nice if five minutes stretched out when you're doing something exciting. But no, the opposite happens! You've probably noticed that when you're having fun, a whole hour can feel like a mere five minutes.

Happenings

How long it takes us to do something depends entirely on how we perceive time. And that has everything to do with what happens to us during that time period. The more things that you experience through a passage of time, the shorter the time would seem to be. That's when people might talk about time flying by. On the other hand, the less you have to do over a given period of time, the longer that time appears to take.

What about tidying up your room? It's obvious. There is not much to do, but it seems to take ages. As if time has slowed to a crawl—if not come to a complete stop.

The Paradox of Time

Now this is where it starts to get crazy, especially when it comes to our memories. It seems that everyday activities like packing bags, tidying up rooms, or taking out the trash not only take forever to get done, they are also quickly forgotten. Yet exciting things like adventures with friends that fly by so quickly can stay in our memories for a long time.

Have You Got a Minute?

Grown-ups have no time. Well, that's what they tell us. They also say that time is money. Oh, and yes, they are very keen to save time. Saving time is an interesting subject. How do you save time? And what can you actually do with the time you saved? Can you buy time? Time that you can use when you need it later? It sounds like a good idea, doesn't it? You could try to save time on boring things like clearing out the dishwasher or taking out the garbage. All this would help you save a great big heap of time. You could then spend that time together. Unfortunately, it does not work that way. Even if we humans always manage to come up with new ways to save time.

At the Same Time

Just checking something online. Oh, a new message!
You need to read it quickly. And also write a swift reply.
Oh, he's online, too. Then he can still sort of . . . get that
thing for me. And now I cannot remember what it is.
Nowadays, people do lots of things at the same time,
so much so that sometimes they don't seem to be fully
present (Hello? Anybody home? Earth to Jane!) They
still manage to get a lot done. Yet often they won't
remember what they did a short while later. Which isn't
that funny if you think about it—have you ever tried to
talk to someone when they were doing something else
at the same time?

What a Strange Time

Studies show that people can now
accomplish much more in the same
period of time than they did in the past.
Strangely, we don't use the time that's
saved to rest or relax. Instead, we try to
get even more done in that saved time.
Then, if we have any time left over, we
fill it by complaining that we don't have
enough time and try to invent more
time-saving devices!
Maybe we're wasting time trying to
save time. It might be true that we all
have plenty of time to spare. It's just a
matter of changing our expectations
to see it—by changing what we want to
achieve in life.

Birds, Bees, and Bloom

Measuring time is a human obsession. Countless inventions help us calculate time and organize ourselves accordingly. But what about animals and plants? How do they cope without watches, apps, and calendars? Animals seem to have a very precise internal clock that tells them when it's time to hunt for food, find a mate, migrate, pollinate, and hibernate.

Humming-bird

Hummingbirds remember the exact time a flower produces fresh nectar. And they wait until the nectar has been topped up—not when the "glass" is half empty!

Bees

Bees remember places and regularly update their inner calendar when flowers are about to blossom.

Fly

A fly's eye can see three times as many images per second than those of humans. Thanks to this slow-motion effect, time flies more slowly for these elusive escape artists!

Pig

Pigs are fanatics when it comes to order. Eat, play, and sleep. But it has to be at the same time every day. Otherwise they'll make quite a stink!

Migratory birds

Migratory birds have built-in alarm clocks and navigation systems. Even orphaned cuckoos know when to fly south and where to go.

Birds

Males sing in spring to attract females. Birds also sing in turns. Early birds like the common redstart step up to the mic eighty minutes before sunrise, while the chaffinch sleeps in until ten minutes before sunrise. There is one rule all birds follow—do not oversleep, otherwise others get to sing first!

Meerkat

Meerkats can sense when it's time to hibernate. When it's time to sleep, they sleep. It doesn't matter whether it's warm or cold. Animals that hibernate rely on their precise internal clock to survive long periods when there is not much food about.

Cicadas

Some species of cicadas only hatch every thirteen or seventeen years. When they do, millions and millions of adults suddenly appear, so many that their natural predators don't have stomachs big enough to eat them all, ensuring the survival of the species.

Tick-Tock Bloom

Flowers and insects complement each other quite well. Flowers bloom one after the other so that their pollinators do not have to pollinate them all at once. The great Swedish natural scientist, Carl Linnaeus, developed a flower clock by observing the opening patterns of flowers. One look at a flower that was about to bloom was all he needed to know the time.

Flowers and When They Bloom

Field Marigold
Between nine and ten in the morning.

Scarlet Pimpernel
After lunchtime, between one and two in the afternoon.

Tiger Lily
At ten in the morning.

Water Lily
This early riser blooms between six and seven in the morning.

Centaury
Nine in the morning

Ice Plant
At ten in the morning.

Chicory
Glows a beautiful blue around three in the afternoon.

St. John's Wort
Between seven and eight in the morning.

Evening Primrose
Comes to life between five and six in the evening.

Tunic Flower
At one in the afternoon.

Red Hawkweed
About three in the afternoon.

Mirabilis Jalapa
Between four and five in the afternoon.

11
12
1
10
2
9
3
8
4
7
5
6

Around the Year

Finding Time in the Sun, Moon, and Stars

For millennia, there was no need for watches, alarm clocks, or phones. You simply got up when the sun rose. The day was over when the sun set, even if you wanted to tell stories for a while by candlelight.

Stargazers

Not every day was like the other. All around the world people divided time into separate sections. These sections were then split into smaller parts which were divided into even smaller parts. This is why different calendars have different lengths of years, months, and weeks. But all calendars, whether Hebrew or Roman, had the same purpose. They were used to calculate when spring began, when it was time to plant crops, and when it was time to harvest. These were also times to celebrate, something people have gathered to do since the dawn of time.

The Trundholm Sun Chariot

A farmer from Denmark discovered this sun chariot dating from 1,400 BCE while plowing his field. Researchers closely examined the marks and suggested that the chariot was used as a 360-day calendar.

Seasons

Today, we know that seasons exist because the earth rotates around the sun. It takes one year for the earth to complete a rotation around the sun. Because the earth is slightly tilted, one side of the earth is always a bit closer to the sun than the other side. That is why we have the changing seasons (the part closest to the sun will be warm with summer and the part furthest from the sun will buckle down for winter). People did not really know about this until a short time ago. Meanwhile, they needed to calculate four specific days to mark the seasons, plant and harvest crops, and celebrate the cycles of life.

Winter Solstice in December

When the sun shines directly over the Tropic of Capricorn, the northern hemisphere is at its farthest from the sun, which is why the night of December 21st is the longest of the year. Many cultures celebrate the Festival of Lights around this date.

Equinox in September

Between September 20th and 22nd, the southern hemisphere moves closer to the sun. Spring has sprung in the southern hemisphere and leaves are beginning to change color in the northern hemisphere. Many northern cultures celebrate Thanksgiving Day to show gratitude to their respective gods for the gifts of summer.

Spring Equinox

On this day, the earth is facing the sun in such a way that both hemispheres (the top and bottom halves of our planet) get equal amounts of sun. From this point on, the northern hemisphere of the earth is closer to the sun and the southern hemisphere is farther away. This means that it will be spring in the northern hemisphere. The beginning of spring is celebrated in many different cultures. Iran, for example, celebrates Nowruz, their New Year, on the first day of spring (March 20th or 21st).

Summer Solstice in June

The summer solstice falls on the 20th, 21st, or 22nd of June. On this day—the longest in the northern hemisphere—the sun shines directly over the Tropic of Cancer. For the rest of the summer, the sun never sets in the North Pole. This is also the day when a spectacular sunrise can be seen at the Stonehenge monuments, a ring of ancient stones in England.

Calculations Using the Moon

The sun has surely always been fascinating. Many cultures even worship it like a god, like Amaterasu in Japan, a goddess who embodies light and sun. However, astronomers also had their eyes set on the moon when it waxed and waned at regular intervals. People calculated that the time from one new moon to the next should always be 29.5 days.

Quite a few calendars, such as the Islamic one, are based on these moon phases. Our months are linked with the moon, although they have thirty or thirty-one days and do not begin with a new moon. If we didn't organize the year by months, you might plan to meet a friend on day 273 of the year instead of September 30th!

Four-Part Moon

The Babylonians, an ancient society that reigned in what is now Iraq, reduced the length of the month to twenty-eight days and then divided it into four equal parts, originating the seven-day week! This also meant that the Babylonian ruler had to decree a leap month every year to align the calendar with the earth's revolution around the sun.

The Planetary Week

Every week, therefore, is a quarter of the moon. Most of the days of the week, however, are not named after the moon, but after other planets. The Babylonians were the first to do this and the Romans followed suit. The Germanic peoples continued the concept, though they replaced the old names of the planets with the names of their own respective planetary gods.

The Names of the Weekdays

Saturn

Venus

Friday

Friday is not connected to the word "free," rather it comes from the Germanic goddess Freyja, who corresponds with the Roman goddess Venus, whose legacy continues in the French *vendredi*, the Spanish *viernes*, and the Italian *venerdi*.

Jupiter

Saturday

Saturday is an exception. It comes from Sabbath, the Jewish day of rest, best recognized in the Italian *sabato* and the Spanish *sábado*. The Romans named Saturday after Saturn. This also corresponds to the English Saturday.

Lord's day

Sunday

Sunday is the day of the sun, from the German Sonntag. However, most romance languages name Sunday after the Latin for "Lord's day," as in the French *dimanche*, the Italian *domenica*, and the Spanish *domingo*.

Luna

Monday

Monday is indeed named after the moon. Moon in Latin is *luna*, so the Romans named Monday *lunae*. The French word for Monday, *lundi*, sounds very similar, as does the Spanish word *lunes*, which definitely sounds like the Roman name.

Tuesday

The Romans decided to name Tuesday after the planet Mars. The French word *mardi* sounds very similar, as does the Spanish *martes*.

Mars

Thursday

The Germanic god Thor is the equivalent of Jupiter, the god after which the Romans named Thursday. Thor survives in the German word *Donnerstag* and in the English *Thursday*, while Jupiter lives on in the French *jeudi*, the Spanish *jueves*, and in the Italian *giovedi*.

Wednesday

The Romans named Wednesday after the planet Mercury, which is reflected in the French *mercredi*, the Italian *mercoledi*, and the Spanish *miércolas*. The Germanic version of the god Mercury was Woden, which is where Wednesday comes from.

Mercury

Three in One Sweep!

The first advanced civilization to develop a calendar with 365 days were the Maya, who were sophisticated observers of the sky and the universe. Thanks to their observations, they knew exactly when to plant crops and when to harvest. They could tell when an eclipse of the sun or moon would take place. They even designed a temple to create a stunning show of light and shadow with the sun during the winter and summer solstices.

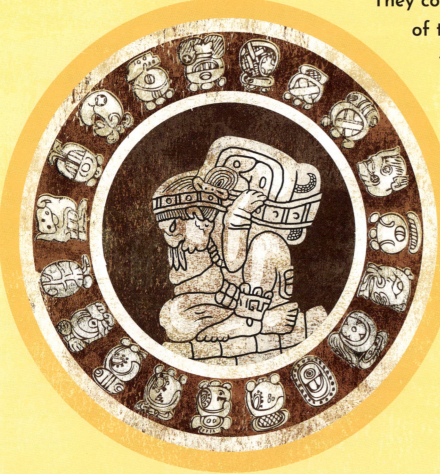

Astronomical Wonder of the World

The pyramid *El Castillo*, built between the ninth and twelfth centuries CE, was a temple to the serpent god Kukulcan. It also functioned as a calendar, and twice a year, on the winter and summer solstices, the rising sun creates a spectacular dance of shadow and light on the temple's north side that looks like a shadowy serpent slowly descending the temple's ninety-one steps. The temple was named one of the New Seven Wonders of the World in 2007.

The Calendar of the Maya

Nowadays, it seems almost incredible that the Maya were the first advanced civilization to develop and use three calendars at the same time. But there were many festivals to celebrate, people to feed, and fields to harvest. All these needed calendars, which were used until the sixteenth century, when the Spanish conquered the Maya.

The Haab Calendar

The Maya calendar for everyday life and agriculture was called Haab. It had, just like our calendar, 365 days. However, the Maya divided the year into eighteen months of twenty days each. That accounted for 360 days. The five days left over were called "the nameless days" and considered very unlucky.

The Tzolkin Calendar for Religious Festivals

The Maya also developed a second calendar to keep track of religious and ceremonial events. The Tzolkin calendar is organized into twenty periods, each of which were thirteen days long, totaling a Tzolkin cycle of 260 days.

The Maya combined the Haab and Tzolkin calendars to create a total of 18,980 unique days equal to fifty-two years, a period of time known as the Calendar Round. It was believed that when a Mayan turned fifty-two years old, they acquired the special wisdom of an elder.

The Long Count

Besides the Haab and Tzolkin calendars, the Maya also developed an even longer calendar for the recording of history. This Long Count calendar is chronological like our current Gregorian calendar and began on August 11, 3114 BCE.

The Gregorian Calendar

The Maya calendar is still used today by their descendants in Guatemala and Honduras. There are several other calendar systems elsewhere in the world that are many centuries and millennia old. In everyday life, however, the Gregorian calendar is used almost everywhere, which is very handy. Otherwise, if you were to travel to another country that used a different calendar, you might be confused what day it was.

The Calendar of the Pope

Today's calendar is called the Gregorian calendar because it was officially introduced by Pope Gregory XIII (1502–1585), an advocate of science, in 1582. However, the Pope did not invent the calendar. The astronomer Aloysius Lilius (1510–1576) first proposed the Gregorian calendar and mathematician Christophorus Clavius (1538–1612) strongly defended it. The Gregorian calendar improved a calendar that the Romans had invented many centuries earlier.

The Roman Miscalculation

The original Roman calendar only had ten months and began the New Year in March. That meant a year was only 304 days. That left the Romans sixty-one days of winter without any months to account for it!

Names of the Months

Emperors have tried again and again to name months after themselves. Julius Caesar and Emperor Augustus had lasting success. Emperor Nero renamed April to Neroneus, but that was quickly dropped after his death. However, the Romans never changed the wrong way to count from September to December. Nor did the pope, and that's why September, October, November, and December are actually wrongly named …

1 Ianuarius
- Named after Janus, the god of beginnings.
- Added after the Republican calendar reform.

2 Februarius
- Named after Februa, the Roman festival of purification or cleaning.
- Added after the Republican calendar reform.

3 Martius
- Named after Mars, the Roman god of war.
- The Roman year originally began with Martius.

4 Aprilis
- Aprilis probably refers to Aphrodite, the Roman goddess of beauty.

5 Maius
- Probably named after Maia, the Roman goddess of growth.

6 Iunius
- Named after Juno, the Roman goddess of marriage and childbirth.

7 Quintilis
- Latin for "fifth," as it was originally the fifth month of the Roman calendar.
- After the Julian calendar reform, Quintilis was changed to Julius, in honor of Julius Caesar.

8 Sextilis
- Derived from the Latin word *sextus* ("sixth"). Originally the sixth month of the calendar.
- Renamed after Emperor Augustus.

9 September
- Derived from the Latin root *septem* ("seventh"). Originally it was the seventh month of the calendar.

10 October
- Derived from the Latin word *octo* ("eight"). Originally it was the eighth month of the calendar.

11 November
- Derived from the Latin word *novem* ("nine"). Originally the ninth month of the calendar.

12 December
- Derived from the Latin word *decem* ("ten"), because it was originally the tenth month of the calendar.

Once Around the Sun

The Gregorian calendar and its predecessor, the Julian calendar, named after Julius Caesar, are solar calendars, which are based on the time it takes the earth to revolve once around the sun. However, that is only an approximation. One year has exactly 365 days in the Gregorian calendar. In fact, it takes the earth 365 days and six hours to complete one revolution around the sun. It may not sound like a big difference, but it adds up over time. If no adjustments were made to the calendar, after a hundred years those six hours would add up to twenty-four days and the beginning of spring would start in April.

Leap Years

For the beginning of spring to always fall on the same date and for the seasons to not drift over the years, a day was added to the calendar every four years. February 29th gave these leap years 366 days instead of 365. But more tweaks were needed. Otherwise, after 128 years, the calendar would deviate by one day from the true solar year, two days after 256 years, and so on. Since the calendar was meant to work for thousands of years, even stricter leap year rules were needed.

Leap Year Rules

The Gregorian calendar introduced the following rules for leap years:

1. Leap years must be divisible by 4.
2. If a year is divisible by both 4 and 100, then it means that the year is not a leap year.
3. If a year is divisible by 4, 100, and 400, it is a leap year.

Got it?

2020 is a leap year according to Rule 1. Clear. Following Rule 2, the year 2100 is not a leap year because it is divisible by both 4 and 100. According to Rule 3, the year 2000 was a leap year because it was divisible by 4, 100, and 400. These rules might seem a little confusing but they are very effective. The Gregorian calendar deviates by only one day from the astronomical solar year every 3,236 years—something we'll have to address when the time comes.

Leap Year Kids—Forever Young

Leaplings are children who were born on the February 29th, which is a day that will not happen again for the next three years. Of course, having a birthday every four years sounds silly. Most leaplings just celebrate in normal years and can choose whether they have their birthday on February 28th or March 1st. Some make a joke about it and are happy to blow only three candles out on their twelfth birthday. The older leaplings get the greater the age gap with children born in common years. If the same age friends are already seventy-two years old, the leapling kid would be just eighteen.

Lunar Years

Centuries ago, cultures that were very close to nature found a way to measure time by counting the twelve full moons. For the Native American Algonquin, each full moon had its own name and described what was going on in the year.

1. Wolf moon
(January)

Because it is so cold and food is in short supply, the hungry wolves howl outside.

2. Snow moon
(February)

Because the snow is thickest at this time of year.

11. Beaver moon
(November)

As beavers busily prepared for winter, Native Americans busily trapped beavers for their warm fur.

12. Cold moon
(December)

As winter deepens and the nights lengthen, cold seeps through the cracks and into the bones.

10. Hunter's moon or Harvest moon
(October)

This is one of the best times to hunt for deer and fox and other animals. When the autumnal equinox occurs in October, this moon is also known as Harvest moon.

4. Pink moon
(April)

The pink moon takes its name from the pink flowers (phlox) that are now blooming.

5. Flower moon
(May)

Flowers are in bloom everywhere.

3. Worm moon
(March)

Once the snow melts, birds can feast on worms again.

6. Strawberry moon
(June)

Delicious strawberries ripen this time of year.

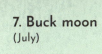

7. Buck moon
(July)

Male deer begin to grow antlers this time of year.

8. Sturgeon moon
(August)

At this time of year, the lakes teem with schools of this fish.

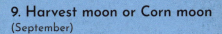

9. Harvest moon or Corn moon
(September)

This was the time to harvest crops like corn and squash, which is why it was also called the Corn moon.

The Year in Judaism

In the two major religions of Judaism and Islam, the time span between new moons is the basis for calculating the calendar year. In the Hebrew and in the Islamic calendar the time span of a new moon until the next one is the basis for calculating year.

A Little Less ...

The Hebrew calendar is used to follow Jewish religious observances. It is lunisolar, which means it is directed by both the moon (*luni*) and sun (*solar*). Not a simple thing to understand. However, it can be worked out if you apply a bit of math. Let's take a look! Each moon phase is 29.5 days long. The Hebrew calendar solves the half-day problem by alternating 29-day months with 30-day months, which averages out to exactly 29.5 days. So far so good. The only problem is that 12 months with 29.5 days equals a year with only 354 days. Such a "normal year" in the Hebrew calendar is 11 days shorter than the solar year with 365 days. So, how do we sort that out?

... and a Little Bit More ...

First, maybe a year does not need to have twelve months. If a thirteenth month could be added on every two or three years, it's fine for the other years to be a bit shorter. That means the He-brew calendar adds a whole leap month every few years, not just a leap day like the Gregorian calendar. With the help of this leap month, the Hebrew calendar is able to bring into line both the moon and the sun, as well as all Jewish religious observances.

... Is Exactly Right!

Passover, for example, is one of the most important Jewish holidays. It originally began as a spring festival but now celebrates the Exodus of Israelites from Egypt and the end of their slavery. Passover always starts on the same day, the 15th day of the Hebrew month of Nisan. What day is this in the Gregorian calendar? Well, sometimes it's in March, sometimes it's in April. It's a bit different every year because the two calendars clearly do not agree with each other.

Miles Ahead of the Christian Calendar

The Gregorian calendar begins after the birth of Christ. The Hebrew calendar begins on a date biblically calculated as the day of creation. This means the year 2020 on the Gregorian calendar is the year 5780 in the Hebrew calendar. In Israel, where many people of the Jewish faith live, the Gregorian calendar is used in everyday life, while the Hebrew calendar is followed to determine the religious holidays and ceremonies.

The Hebrew Calendar

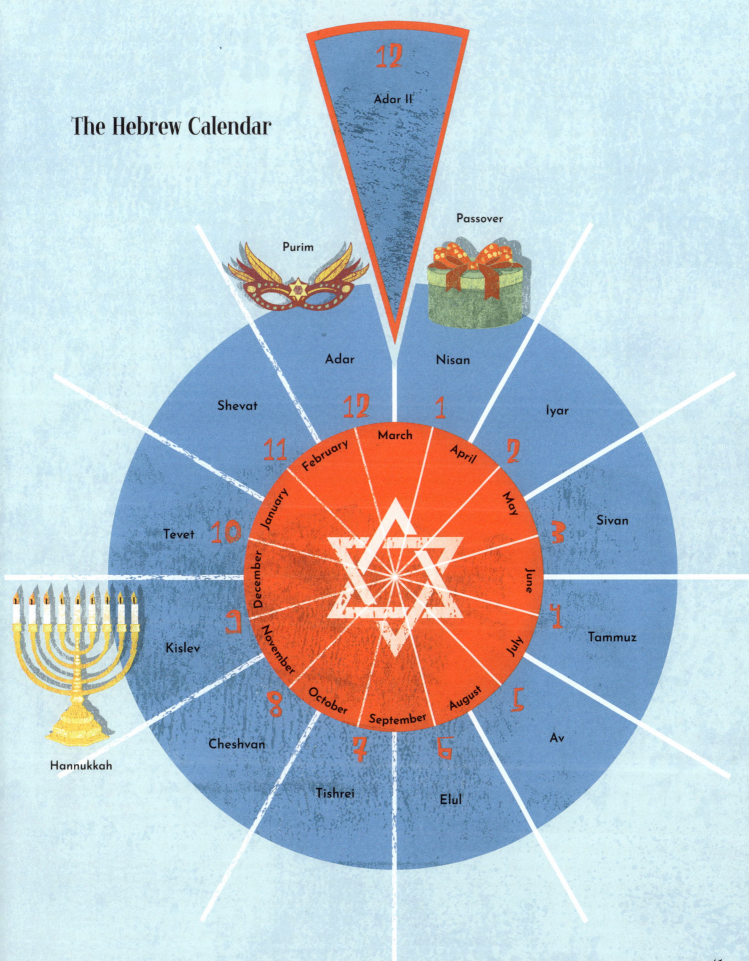

Islamic Calendar

The moon is still an important symbol in countries where Islam plays a major role. For example, in Turkey and in many Arab countries, the international aid agency is called Red Crescent and not Red Cross. On many flags, you can see a crescent moon as well.

Everything Starts in Medina

Muhammad is the founder of Islam. In 622 CE, he fled his persecutors in Mecca and escaped to Medina. This moment is considered the beginning of the Islamic calendar. Therefore, according to the Islamic calendar, we are not in the twenty-first but in the fifteenth century.

622 CE = 0
2020 CE = 1441/1442

Short Years

Unlike the Hebrew calendar, the Islamic or Hijiri calendar is based exclusively on the moon. The sun does not matter here. What usually happens is you wait for a scholar to notice the thin new crescent in the sky every month. Only then does the new month begin. Depending on the weather, this sometimes happens after twenty-nine or thirty days. Because the year in the Islamic calendar is a true lunar year, it is eleven days shorter than the Gregorian year. So even though the Gregorian calendar has a "head start" by over six hundred years, the Islamic calendar will eventually catch up to it in the year 20874, when it will actually take over the lead.

Celebration Months

In Islam, some months are especially significant. For example, Ramadan is the ninth month of the calendar. Adolescent and adult Muslims fast throughout the day. But because the Islamic years are so short compared to the Gregorian year, Ramadan does not always take place at the same time of year like Easter or Passover. In fact, this month of fasting moves backward on the Gregorian calendar as the years roll by. In 2015 it came in June, but in 2020 it will be observed in April, and by 2030 it will occur in January.

Generations

In the past, religious holidays used to be the central events of our lives. And complicated calendars were invented to keep track of them. On these special days you went to church instead of school and celebrated with your family or with the whole village. Today, we like an occasional day off from school, but our lives have become more scattered and private. Our uncle and his friend live far away in the big city. A cousin may practice a different faith. Maybe we do not believe in any god, or mom has to work despite the holiday, and our brother would rather go camping with his friends. Or maybe the only way to get everyone together is through FaceTime or Skype!

Calendar of Life

Nowadays we celebrate festivals of different religions together. In some schools, students dress up for Carnival, Halloween, the Mexican Day of the Dead, or the Jewish Purim. Of course, we also celebrate events that have nothing to do with religion, such as birthdays and anniversaries. Family calendars, diaries, photo albums, or social media platforms now serve as our calendars of life, reminding us of our important days.

Generation XYZ

In today's society, life is measured in generations. Whoever goes into the same school year with someone belongs to the same generation, including those who are a few years younger or a few years older. Parents, on the other hand, are part of a completely different generation and so are grandparents. People of one generation often grow up with similar hairstyles and listen to the same music. They also experience political events together and participate in similar social issues. Most of the time, three to four generations of a family are alive at the same time. The world record is seven: in 1989, a 109-year-old woman became a great-great-grandmother. Family trees come in many different forms. You can easily do one yourself.

Meryem's Family Tree

Bonnie

Grandma Bonnie is actually not my grandma at all, but the mother of Thomas, my mother's ex-husband. But step-grandma doesn't sound too nice, which she is—really nice.

Willy

Louise

Thomas

My mother's ex-husband and Jacob's dad. And Olivia's grandpa. And me? Well, I've no idea. I just call him Thomas.

David

My favorite uncle. And even if grandpa says that he is not really my uncle but "only" my brother-in-law by marriage to my brother. I don't care, to me he is still my uncle.

Olivia

My little niece. I love her. And I am her aunt. Crazy, isn't it? I am only 11.

Jacob

My half-brother. But I only say that when I am mad at him, which rarely happens because we do not live together anymore. Unfortunately, Jacob is much older than me and we have the same mother, but not the same father. Jacob is even a father himself. I think that's cool!

Grandpa Daniel is my mother's father and the grandpa of Jacob and me. He does not talk much when we visit him, but he is always playing cards with my dad.

Yusra

Grandma Yusra used to look after me a lot when I was small. We speak in Turkish with each other. That makes her happy.

Daniel

Ali

Grandpa Ali always laughs. He is the nicest grandpa in the world.

Clementine

My mother. She used to be married to Thomas, Jacob's father. But now she is married to my father, Ibrahim. Thankfully. Otherwise I would not be here.

Ibrahim

My father. But I call him Baba. It sounds nicer. It is the Turkish word for father. Baba talks in Turkish with me, I talk English with him.

Aliyah

Aliyah is my aunt. She is my dad's sister. Baba and Aliyah don't always see eye to eye. But I like her a lot. I love staying at her place.

➤ Meryem

Hi! I'm Meryem and this is my family. I have six grandmas and grandpas. Many in my school class say that's not possible, but in our case it's true. And it's very handy when it comes to gifts!

45

Around the Day

47

Clocks for Night and Day

Today, our smartphones and smartwatches tell us when to wake up, when our food is ready, when to pick up our kids, and when we ought to be heading home. It's hard to imagine life without these devices. But the ancient Greeks didn't need them to tell time. How? Simply by looking down at their shadows. At least when there was no sundial nearby.

Be Your Own *Gnomon*!

What on earth is a gnomon? Maybe the Greek god of dwarves? Well, actually no. The word means "shadow caster," as in a long, thin upright rod. When it's hit by the sun's rays, it casts a shadow. You can tell the time depending on the shadow's length. From early morning till noon, the shadow is shorter, and then it lengthens from noon to evening.

If you don't have a tall rod handy, you can always use yourself. Honestly! That is what the ancient Greeks did. They measured the shadow stretching out from their foot, always putting one foot in front of the other. You can try this in midsummer (as long as it's not raining). You'll probably reach about six feet. And be totally on time.

Shadow Casters

Sundials that measure time using a shadow have been around for approximately 5,500 years. The ancient Greeks called them gnomons, the Romans called them solaria. Sundials were widespread throughout the world until it was time for the modern watch to become our main time-teller in the nineteenth century.

Samrat Yantra

The world's largest sundial is in Jaipur, India. Its gnomon is eighty-eight feet high (27 m) and moves about thirteen feet (4 m) per hour. It is accurate to two seconds. Built between 1724 and 1734, it has been a UNESCO World Heritage Site since 2010.

Please Be Punctual!

When it was evening or dark, the sundial was not really of much use. Most people did not have a problem with that. When there was no longer any sunlight, it meant it was the end of the working day.

In earlier times, Christian monks could get quite stressed about time. They prayed, studied, and worked at strictly regulated times. It was important not to oversleep. This is why they divided the night into twelve hours and invented different clocks to indicate how time passed.

Candle Timers

The monks marked candles with lines. When the candle burned down beyond a line, it meant that an hour had passed. However, this was not practical if you fell asleep. So the monks stuck pebbles or nails into the candles, which would then fall to the floor whenever an hour passed. They hoped that the noise from the falling pebble would wake them up.

Hourglasses

In the fourteenth century, monks utilized another handy timekeeping tool—the hourglass. Turn once, then pray. Turn three times for study time, then off to work and please do not forget to turn the hourglass again. Oftentimes, a single monk used to stay awake at night turning the hourglass at regular intervals. That sounds pretty exhausting!

Smoking Dragons

Buddhist monks in China and Japan faired a little better. And that is because people in China invented an incense timekeeper. Inside the belly of this "dragon" was a burning incense stick. Above it was hung a thread divided at intervals by balls that dropped as the thread gradually burned away. The sound of the ball dropping would help keep the meditating monks alert, or wake them up if they had fallen asleep!

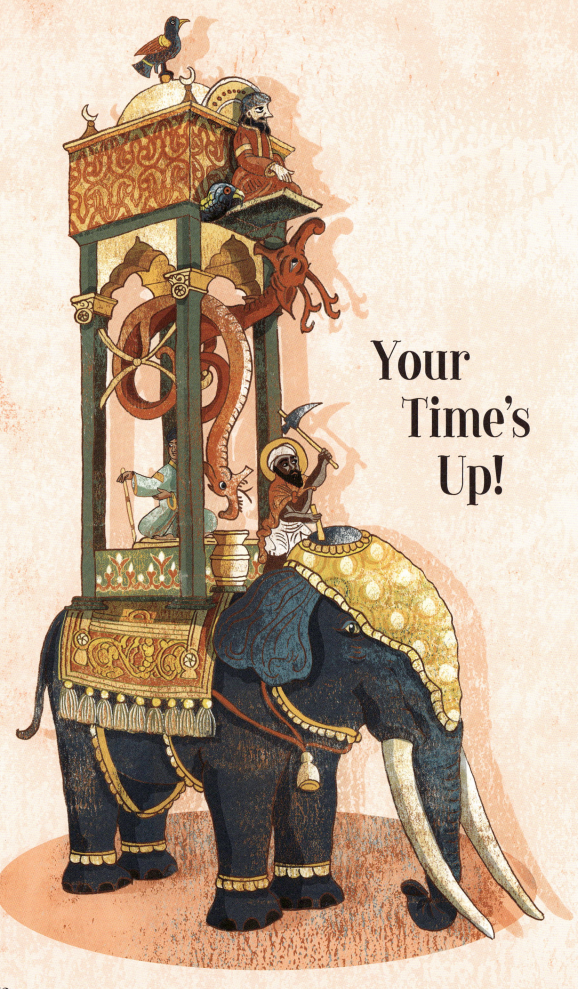

Your
Time's
Up!

In ancient Greece and Rome, public debates were a central part of the culture. Every speaker was given equal time to convince others of his opinion. Sundials were dependent on clear skies and didn't work indoors. A new form of timekeeping was needed.

Water Clocks

Water clocks were the first timekeepers that did not need the sun. Originally invented by the ancient Egyptians, and possibly ancient China, the ancient Greeks and Romans developed more reliable and accurate water clocks. Clepsydra, as it was called by the ancient Greeks, meant "water thief." They felt that time was being stolen from them.

Water clocks could measure how much time has passed, but not how late it was in the day. However, a special water clock automat came close to do so.

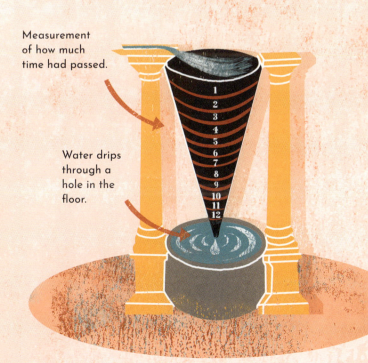

Measurement of how much time had passed.

Water drips through a hole in the floor.

The Elephant Clock

One of the world's most famous water clocks is the elephant clock devised by the Muslim engineer Ismail al-Jazari in the twelfth century.

Every thirty minutes, a floating bowl sinks in a tank of water inside the elephant's belly, triggering the phoenix to whirl about on top of the tower, releasing a metal ball that falls from a falcon's beak into the dragon's mouth. The dragon then drops the ball into the vase below, which triggers the mahout (elephant rider) to strike a cymbal with his mallet, signaling the half hour. The hour is shown on the half-disc at the top of the clock while the minutes are shown by the scribe sitting on the elephant's back. All this is done without springs or a pendulum as they had not yet been invented. Al-Jazari wrote such an accurate guide to the design of the elephant clock in *The Book of Knowledge of Ingenious Mechanical Devices* that it can easily be replicated today. In fact, you can visit life-size copies in Dubai and in Switzerland!

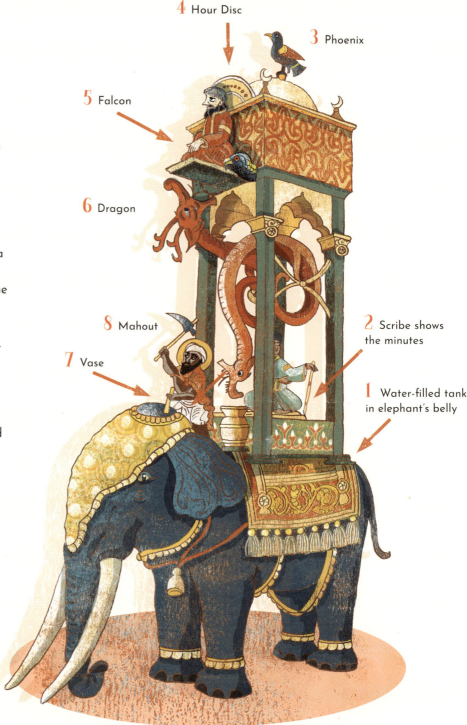

4 Hour Disc

3 Phoenix

5 Falcon

6 Dragon

8 Mahout

7 Vase

2 Scribe shows the minutes

1 Water-filled tank in elephant's belly

This timekeeping masterpiece by Ismail al-Jazari brings many different cultures together. The elephant represents Indian and African cultures and carries two Arabian figures. Egyptian culture is represented by the rising phoenix, Greek by the vases, Persian by the rug, and China by the two dragons. The elephant clock beautifully represents al-Jazari's inclusive view of the world.

Ismail al-Jazari (1136–1206) was a Muslim scholar, engineer, and inventor, among many other disciplines.

54

How Does the Clock Work?

1

A water tank (1) is hidden in the elephant's belly. A bowl with a small hole floats on the water. As it slowly fills up and sinks, it pulls ropes that are attached to the bowl.

2

One of the ropes is connected to the scribe (2). The gradual sinking of the bowl causes the scribe's pen to indicate the minutes.

3

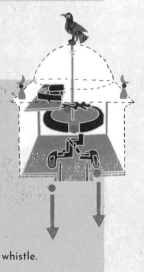

When the bowl is full and sinks to the bottom of the tank, it pulls on another rope that releases a metal ball in the clock's dome that hits a fan that, causing the phoenix to spin and whistle.

4

The hour disc (4) continues to rotate with the fan. It has 12 circles. Each circle represents an hour. And with every half hour, a half circle is added.

5-8

The ball rolls from the fan to the falcon (5), who spits the ball into the waiting mouth of the dragon (6). The weight of the ball causes the dragon to drop the ball into a vase (7) that triggers the mahout (8) to hit a cymbal with his mallets. Half an hour is up!

The moment the dragon (6) tilts downward, another rope in the elephant's belly pulls the bowl back up again to start the process all over. Once a day, the metal balls need to be returned to the dome.

And Now for Some Noise!

Have you ever stood next to a church when the bells were ringing? It's really loud. And that's the way it was meant to be, especially back in the Middle Ages when bells needed to be heard far and wide. As more people began living in towns to work as merchants and tradespeople, church bells helped them keep track of time. Though the bells rang only on the hour, it was enough for people to know if they were running late or had more time to get where they were going or finish what they were doing.

How Long Does an Hour Actually Take?

It depended a lot on the seasons of the year. During the Middle Ages, the day was split into two halves—day and night—divided into twelve hours each. But the length of each hour changed with the seasons, so that in the summer daytime hours were longer and nighttime hours shorter. That meant daytime hours could be stretched to eighty minutes, while they were shortened to forty minutes during the winter months. In spring and fall, when both halves were about the same, an hour would work out to sixty minutes.
This system began to change at the beginning of the fourteenth century with the advent of the mechanical clock.
From then on the length of the hour was the same no matter what season it was.

Early Mechanical Clocks

The first clocks to not rely on sun, water, or fire appeared at the beginning of the fourteenth century. They did, however, need lots of room and people to regularly look after them. They also needed a rope, a weight, a roller, a gear train, a clock hand, and a dial. Oh, and a new invention: a verge escapement.

Early Mechanical Clocks Worked Like This:

A rope is wrapped around a cylinder and a weight is hung on the rope. Gravity pulls the weight down and causes a roller to move. The roller is connected to a gear train, which sets off the clock hand. The hand moves across the dial, showing the time in hours (the minute hand had not yet been invented). To stop the weight from simply sliding off the rope, there was a verge escapement. This enabled the movement to be slowed down and evenly regulated. The oldest mechanical clock that is still working today can be found at the Salisbury Cathedral in England. It is believed to have been in existence since 1386.

The Invention of the Pendulum Clock

The next stage in the development of the mechanical clock took place after Galileo Galilei (1564-1642) focused his scientific mind on the movements of the pendulum at the end of the sixteenth century. His law of the pendulum can easily be put the test.

fast

slow

Galileo Galilei's Law of the Pendulum

If you dangle a weight, then the time for that weight to swing is dependent on the length of the mount. Large pendulums take longer to swing, short ones swing faster. If you make a pendulum four times longer it will only swing half as quickly as before.

Sensitive but Successful Clock

The Dutch natural scientist, Christiaan Huygens (1629-1695), invented the first pendulum clock in 1657. It was a resounding success because the steady swing of the pendulum made it much more accurate. It was, however, a little bit sensitive. There were initially some problems with changes in temperature and other environmental factors, but it has managed to hold out and keeps on ticking!

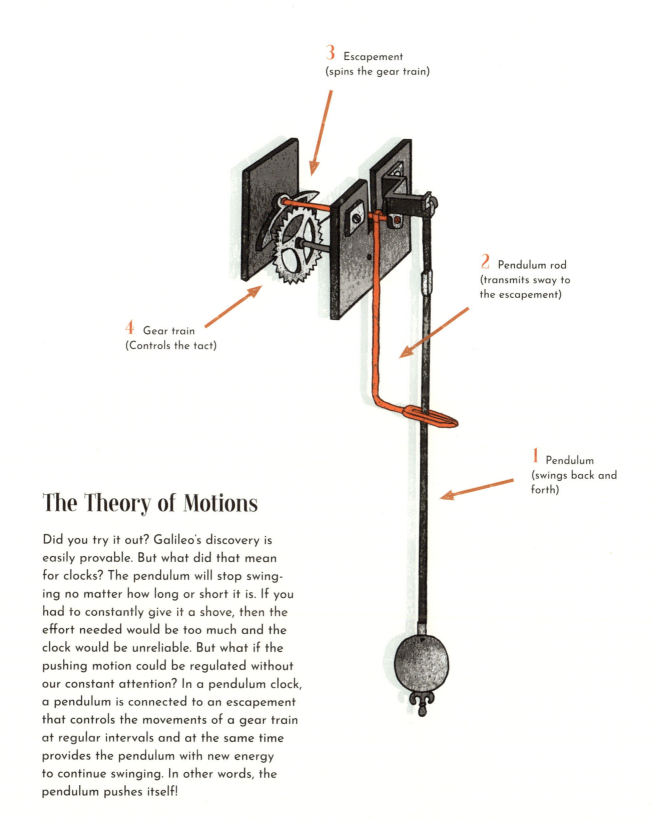

3 Escapement
(spins the gear train)

2 Pendulum rod
(transmits sway to
the escapement)

4 Gear train
(Controls the tact)

1 Pendulum
(swings back and
forth)

The Theory of Motions

Did you try it out? Galileo's discovery is
easily provable. But what did that mean
for clocks? The pendulum will stop swinging no matter how long or short it is. If you
had to constantly give it a shove, then the
effort needed would be too much and the
clock would be unreliable. But what if the
pushing motion could be regulated without
our constant attention? In a pendulum clock,
a pendulum is connected to an escapement
that controls the movements of a gear train
at regular intervals and at the same time
provides the pendulum with new energy
to continue swinging. In other words, the
pendulum pushes itself!

Tell Me the Time and I'll Tell You Where You Are!

At the beginning of the eighteenth century, it was not uncommon for ships to drift about at sea for weeks on end, lost with food supplies running low and diseases breaking out. Some ships even ended up in places that were far off from their intended destinations. On October 22, 1707, four British warships sank off the southwestern coast of England, taking with them about two thousand lives. This was not because they were attacked, but because their officers had miscalculated the positions of the ships. Blinded by fog, they were driven against the cliffs of the Isles of Scilly. It was one of the worst maritime disasters in British naval history.

Long and Wide!

At sea, where there are no street signs, vessels calculate their position on an imaginary grid of lines that covers the planet. The lines of latitude are parallel with the equator (horizontal), while the lines of longitude connect the north and the south poles (vertical). You can describe any location on the planet by latitude and longitude. Let's find out how.

Turns out finding one's latitude is fairly simple. From at least the time of Christopher Columbus (1451–1506), mariners have been able to determine latitude by measuring the angle of the sun during the day or certain stars at night to the horizon. Determining longitude was much more difficult.

The Longitude Act

After the disaster off the Isles of Scilly, the British parliament passed the Longitude Act in 1714, which offered a prize of twenty thousand pounds to anyone who could find a way to determine a ship's longitude. Everyone and anyone tackled the problem. Even astronomers got in on the act. They tried to determine the longitude by observing the position of the moon and its distance to the stars. That was complicated and impossible in bad weather.

Then a carpenter named John Harrison (1693–1776) got involved. He also worked on watches in his spare time. It was clear to him that the longitude could be worked out if you took a clock to sea showing the time of the home port. And that is because longitude is related to time.

Determining Longitude

You need:

- The exact time of the home port, whose longitude is known.
- A navigator who can determine the time onboard by the position of the sun.
- A navigator who can calculate the difference between the time onboard and the time at the home port.

Since the earth turns 360 degrees over a 24-hour period, the difference in time onboard and at the home port tells the navigator the ship's longitude.

What Does that Actually Have to Do with Time?

But first a clock that wasn't affected by the ship's motions and changes in temperature needed to be invented. Pendulum clocks, after all, needed a stable base.

The Marine Chronometer

A clock unaffected by the sea's motions or weather extremes was foremost in John Harrison's mind. In 1735, he finished his first clock to determine the longitude at sea. It was a huge machine that got in everyone's way during the test journey to Lisbon. Nonetheless, it helped the ship safely reach its destination.

H4 | The World's Most Famous Clock

It looks like a pocket watch, doesn't it? At over three pounds, the H4 is really heavy, but it also contains many new inventions. A bimetallic strip, for example, to eliminate problems caused by temperature fluctuations. And even when it needed to be wound up, it lost no time but just carried on working. In 1759, the H4 was ready and tested on many sea journeys. The captains were enthusiastic!

Bad Losers,
Poor Winner

Even though John Harrison had found a reliable way to determine longitude at sea, he never received an official reward because astronomers on the Board of Longitude wanted their moon-distance theory to win. They also believed that a simple carpenter could not come up with a solution that they had failed to find themselves. But his willingness to try out new things enabled him to change the course of history. The famous Captain James Cook took the watch on a trip around the world and wrote about it enthusiastically. In 1772, with King George's support, Harrison received 8,750 pounds from the British parliament, which was quite a lot of money at the time.

Harrison's invention of the marine chronometer made journeys by sea much safer, which opened the way for the rapid expansion of European trade and commerce. To this day ships have chronometers installed alongside modern electronics to help them navigate all bodies of water.

Revolution Number 10

What a lovely clock? But there is something wrong with it. Why are there so many rings with different numbers? And is the number 3 in the wrong place? It is definitely not the only one. What's going on here?

The 100 minutes of a new hour.

The new 10 hours of the day.

The 24 hours of the day in the old system.

The 60 minutes of an old hour.

Stop the Bells from Ringing!

The clock originates from the time of the French Revolution. In 1789, the French people had had enough of kings, popes, and everything that reminded them of the rich and powerful. Revolutionaries stormed a prison called the Bastille and for ten years France was in turmoil until Napoleon overthrew the revolutionary government.
The French Revolution questioned many systems that had long been in place, bringing new ideas into the world, including freedom for all, the abolishment of slavery, and women's rights. It also strongly weakened the influence of the Catholic church, including the way they organized time. Why did an hour have sixty minutes and a minute sixty seconds? Everything seemed to be unreasonable. And impractical arithmetically.

The Revolutionary Calendar

So time was reorganized in France, beginning with a new calendar.
The year still kept its twelve months, but every month now had thirty days spread out over three weeks lasting ten days each. And just like the Maya, five days were added at the end of the year.
The calendar wasn't the only thing revolutionized. Liters, meters, grams, kilograms, and the franc were introduced. To simplify things, ten had become the most important number for calculating all measurements—including time. A day was divided into ten hours. Every hour had one hundred minutes and every minute had one hundred seconds. This meant the new hour took 2.4 hours longer than before.

The Consequences of Time

The French Revolution was very instrumental in the development of democracy. And working with numbers that are divisible by ten led to great progress in many areas. Liters, grams, and kilograms are units of measurement that are still used in Europe today and, until the introduction of the euro, the franc, like the dollar, is based on the metric system of ten, which the French revolutionaries originally created.
But the revolutionary calendar and its new time-keeping system lasted just thirteen years, abolished by Napoleon in 1806. After Napoleon himself was abolished, the French reverted to the old Gregorian seven-day week and the 24-hour clock. Maybe this was because the 100-minute hours and their 100-second minutes had been extremely long. Perhaps it also had something to do with people having a day off every seven rather than ten days.

On Time, More on Time, Extremely Punctual

At some point in time, clocks in towns had become essential. Bakers, butchers, and schools had set opening times. But clock technology wasn't available to everyone yet. Pendulum clocks were not only very large, they were also quite expensive. Which is why people had to go outdoors, walk to the nearest church tower, or listen for the bells to toll to check the time. It wasn't until the end of the eighteenth century that pocket watches became available to the general population.

On a Chain

The pocket watch was powered by a helical or coil spring instead of a pendulum. The first pocket watches only had a single hour hand. Regardless, the actual time of day was now available to more people than ever before. Pocket watch owners proudly wore their shiny timepieces on a chain for all to see.

On the Arm

At the beginning of the twentieth century, some women started tying their pocket watches to their arms. They were laughed at. Then, during the First World War, naval officers realized that it would be more practical to actually wear watches directly on the wrist. This meant your hands were free and you could tell the time at a glance. Consequently, watchmakers began to develop timepieces specifically for marines and pilots.

By the end of the First World War, everyone was captivated by the wristwatch. Wearing one became as essential as putting on shoes. And it stayed that way for a very long time. Right up until the arrival of smartphones. Some people get annoyed nowadays at having to check the time on their phones—with all the various apps they forget to actually check the time. That might explain a renewed interest these days in designer wristwatches.

Frequency Pulses

For thousands of years, time was calculated according to the movements of celestial bodies. Then it was discovered that the earth does not take precisely 24 hours to complete a full turn on its axis. In fact, the earth's rotation has gradually slowed over time. It is now rotating more slowly than ever!

In 1967, the world's scientific community agreed to measure time by the frequency of an atom. The new second equaled 9,192,631,770 pulse frequencies in a caesium-133 atom. It's hard to imagine, but atomic clocks can measure these pulses. There are currently more than 400 atomic clocks globally that keep the International Atomic Time (TAI).

International Atomic Time and Solar Time

This extremely accurate time measurement system is needed, for example, with GPS systems and satellite-controlled aircraft safety. Solar time, on the other hand, which is the time that records the actual length of the earth's day, lags behind International Atomic Time. This is because the earth's rotation is slowing down due to the moon's orbit gradually slowing down. The changes are very small, but they add up: a time will come billions of years from now when the day and month will both equal 47 of our current days! In the meantime, a leap second is added whenever solar and International Atomic Time deviate by 0.9 seconds. A single minute of the day will then be sixty-one instead of sixty seconds long. This occurs once every year and a half. In our day-to-day life, we're too busy to notice.

Rise and Shine!

Sleep late and stay in bed until the sun rises. This is unthinkable for inventors. This very moment they are fiddling about to find new ways of getting people out of bed in the morning. No mercy!

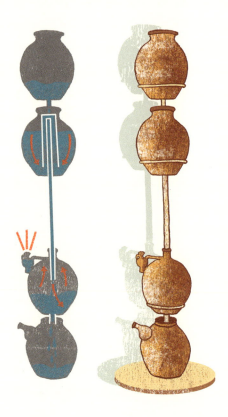

Plato's Alarm Clock

Over 2,400 years ago, the Greek philosopher, Plato, worried about not getting up on time. There were only clocks and sundials in those days. Since he couldn't figure out how to get the sun to make a noise, he built the world's first alarm clock using water, gravity, and three containers or vessels. During the night, water dripped from the top vessel into the second one below. When the second one filled up about seven hours later, the water would pour into a third vessel, rapidly forcing the air inside of it out through a small hole or tube to create an alarm whistle. Once that vessel was filled, the water would empty into the bottom vessel, which would then be ready to set the alarm clock for the next morning.

Feet First into the Day

About five hundred years ago, Leonardo da Vinci (1452-1519) also invented an alarm clock that used water. His device also drained water from one receptacle into another, but instead of an alarm whistle sounding, a series of levers would be activated to suddenly lift his feet in the air and stir him awake.

Groundhog Day

In 1747, Levi Hutchins (1761-1855), an apprentice watchmaker from the state of New Hampshire who had to get up at four in the morning to get to work on time, invented the first American alarm clock. It's only drawback was that it only rang at 4 a.m. and could not be turned off—even on weekends! It would take another hundred years for a French inventor, Antoine Rédier (1817-1954), to design the world's first adjustable alarm.

Sweet Sleep vs. the Alarm Clock

Now that alarm clocks are universal, sleeping in has become a kind of sport for many people. For those of us who outfox our alarm clocks by hitting them and going back to sleep, there are some special inventions, like a throwable alarm clock. Hitting the snooze button is not enough. You have to grab the clock and throw it across the room. If you don't do it hard enough, it continues beeping, forcing you to get out of bed to turn it off. Is this clever? Or a new way to wake up on the wrong side of the bed?

Catch Me If You Can

Clocky is an alarm clock invented by Gauri Nanda in 2005 when she was a student at MIT Media Lab. Clocky is an alarm clock with wheels. It's nice enough to let a sleeper snooze once. But a second snooze sends it rolling off your bedside table and onto the floor, where it will race away in random directions, twittering and beeping and whistling until you have to get out of bed to find it and shut it off. Good morning!

Silent but Effective

By the way, not all alarm clocks make a sound. People with hearing difficulties use alarm clocks similar to Leonardo da Vinci's design. Some are placed under the pillow to vibrate you awake. Others will trigger flashing lights to go off until you wake up.

Curiosities
of Time

Once people had figured out how to measure time without having to look to the skies, there's been no shortage of ambitious, inventive, and imaginative clock designs. These projects have often been incredibly expensive, large, and even absurd. Some clocks were supposed to demonstrate the power of the church or the might of the state. Cities competed with each other to build the biggest clock towers. Some people bought fancy timepieces or had them made to show off their wealth. Just like the Russian ruler Catherine the Great for example, who bought a peacock clock in 1781, which one can still admire in St. Petersburg.

Peacock Clock

It's not quite fair to call this automaton—an early form of robot—a peacock clock because several different animals move about to provide the time: a rooster, an owl, and some squirrels ...
Can you find the mushroom? There is a little dragonfly perched on top of it that rotates as the clock's second hand.
The English goldsmith, James Cox (1723-1800), made the peacock clock in 1772. It is now in the Hermitage Museum in St. Petersburg, Russia. Every Wednesday, the clock is wound up and visitors can marvel at this extraordinary work of art and technology in glorious motion.

It seems that time fascinates people around the world and encourages them to build new and imaginative ways to measure and announce time. You have already seen some special timepieces here in this book. There are a few more in the cabinet of curiosities on the next two pages. Which one do you like best?

Big Ben

In 1859, sixteen horses were required to pull the fifteen-ton Great Bell nicknamed "Big Ben" to the Clock Tower in London's Palace of Westminster. One of the most recognizable symbols of the United Kingdom, it was named a UNESCO World Heritage Site in 1987.

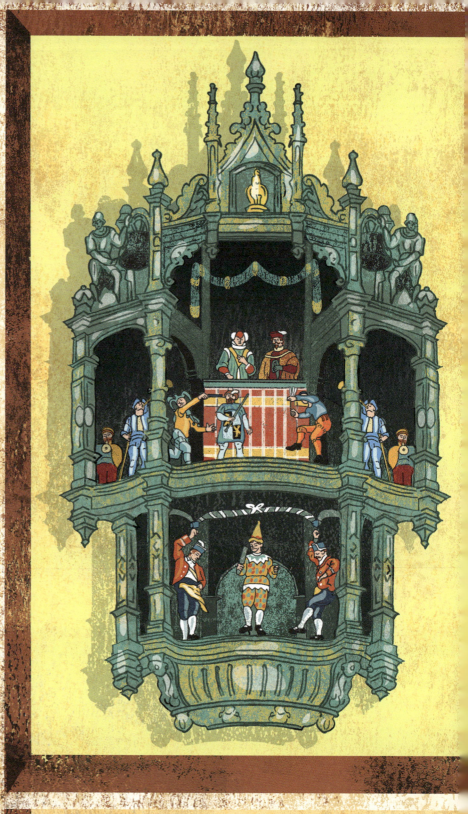

Rathaus-Glockenspiel of Munich

Built in 1908, this famous timepiece chimes twice a day at 11 a.m. and noon. 43 bells ring and 32 figures perform two stories from the sixteenth century. One celebrates a local duke's marriage with a joust between knights on horseback. The other re-enacts a traditional dance.

Cuckoo Clock

Popularized in Germany's Black Forest region during the eighteenth century, the mechanics of cuckoo clocks have remained unchanged ever since. A little house, a little door, a clock face, and a little cuckoo are always parts of this clock. Inside are two bellows attached to whistles that make the famous cuckoo sound.

Balmoral Hotel, Edinburgh

Ever since this famous clock was completed in 1902, it has been set three minutes fast so that passengers won't miss their trains. The only time of year it's accurate is on New Year's Eve!

Noon Gun

There are two cannons atop a mountain in Cape Town, South Africa. Since 1806, one of them fires every day at noon, except Sundays and holidays. The other gun serves as back up. Historically, the guns were fired to announce the arrival of a ship into the city's harbor.

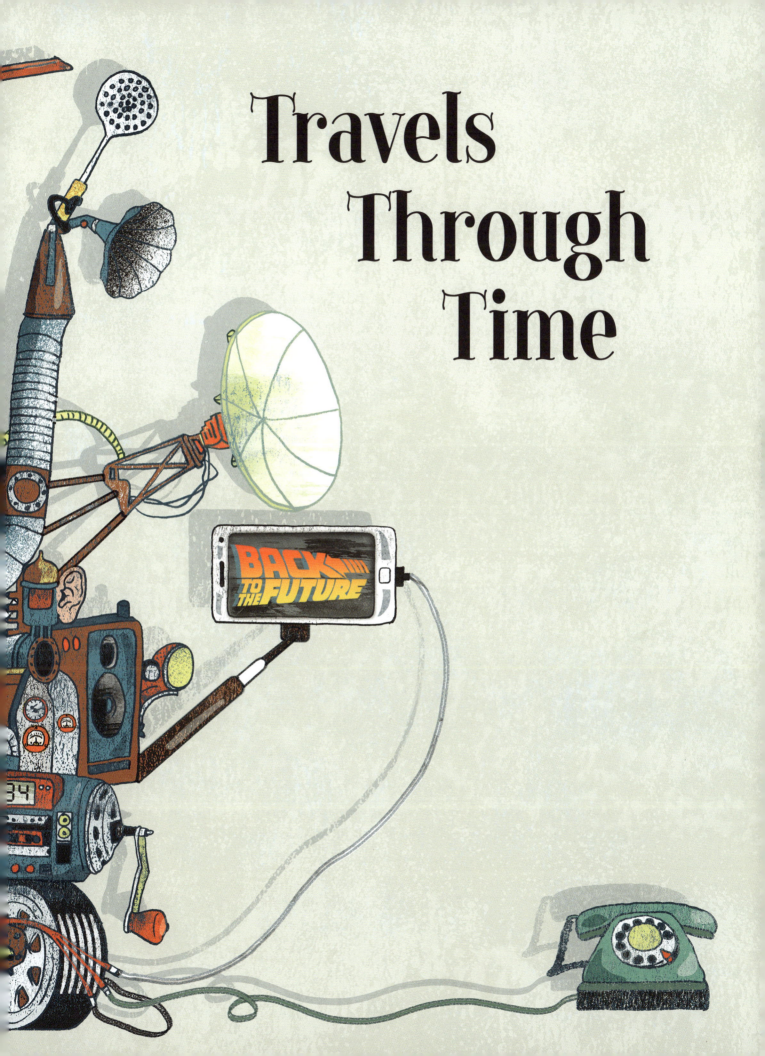

Travels Through Time

The Train Is Lost!

The development of railroads changed everything. Because clocks ran differently everywhere, trains could arrive before they had left, or more time would had passed than a train had actually traveled. At first, railroad planners created their own time and set their own timetables. They mostly used the time of the location where the train was based. As you might expect, this resulted in many slip-ups. Passengers missed their trains or trains never arrived, often because they crashed into each other. Until the nineteenth century, cities and towns around the world went by their own time, so that 1 p.m. in your town would be different from 1 p.m. in my town. Additionally, some places counted the hours down from midnight, some from sunrise, and some from noon. Surprisingly, all these different times didn't create as much confusion as you might imagine.

Local Time = Sun Time

Initially, this business of different local times made total sense. People got their bearings from the sun. In one town, the sun goes up in the east a half hour earlier than a town farther west, so the clocks were a half hour apart. This did not help the men from the railroad one little bit. It was even more complicated in North America because solar times on such a big continent lie many hours apart from each other. Complicating matter further, there were many different railway firms who all had their own times and schedules.

One Clock to Rule Them All

After missing a train in 1876 due to different time schedules, the Canadian railroad engineer, Sandford Fleming (1827-1915), started thinking about fixing this problem. In 1879, he proposed a single 24-hour clock for the entire world with twenty-four time zones to account for local solar times. Each of the twenty-four time zones would differ from the next by one hour. We now know how clever his idea was. But it took a few years for the world to catch up to Fleming's proposal. Then, in 1884, an agreement was reached to establish Greenwich, London, as the world's prime meridian, or the starting point of the world clock. It took a few more years for most countries to accept the time zones. A few countries still deviate from these time zones for political reasons.

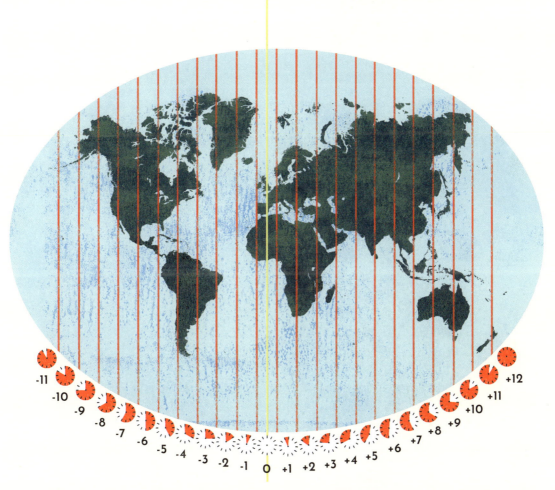

Clocking In and Clocking Out

Time became more and more important toward the end of the nineteenth century. And pretty powerful, too! Working by day had become a thing of the past, especially with the invention of electric light. Now, punctuality had become something of a religion. Those who weren't on time were robbing other people of their time. These time robbers were bad! Well, that was the argument of people who made money out of other people's time.

Time Police

Timepieces accurate to the second were perfect for keeping a watch on people. In 1887, the invention of the time-stamp clock made it possible to monitor who arrived to work on time, who was taking too long of a break, and when people stopped working. Time management in factories had begun and the only thing that mattered was knowing the exact amount of time needed to get a piece of work done. People worked around the clock so that expensive machines could work nonstop. Some people had to work through the night, even if it went against their biological clock.

How Long Does It Take to Turn a Screw?

A man named Frederick Winslow Taylor (1856–1915) made it his business to refine the individual work stages of manufacturing products. For example: 1, grab the screwdriver; 2, tighten the screw; 3, put the screwdriver away again. He then took a stopwatch and set a maximum time that each tiny stage should take. This requirement was exactly what was demanded of the workers. The factory workers were not interested that this was maddeningly boring and that it made people stressed and ill. They were earning good money through this way of working..

Time to Be Happy

For a long time, many factories were working in accordance with Taylor's principles of scientific management—until machines began to take over the work people used to do. A cheaper alternative has been to set up factories in countries where poverty is so extreme that the local people are willing to be controlled by such timekeeping devices. People in wealthier countries tend to disregard strict management by timekeeping machines.

In many larger corporations, however, there are digital ways to manage attendance and timekeeping, creating a culture where people are still seen as hardworking the longer they're clocked in. But what really matters is how quickly and well you get your work done, not how long you sit at your desk. People who aren't slaves to the clock have more time to think about their lives and others and are probably much happier for it.

In his film *Modern Times*, Charlie Chaplin made fun of how people were being controlled by time-stamp clocks and stopwatches.

Theories about Time

Watchmakers and railroad and factory owners were not the only ones interested in time. Philosophers thought about time from the very beginning. In a way, it is almost part of their job to think about how times works. The philosopher and theologian, Augustine (354-430), did not find it so easy. "What is, after all, time?" he wondered. "If nobody asks me about it, I know, but when I explain it to them, then I do not."

In the last few centuries, some mathematicians and physicists have had some real big fights about time. These arguments continue to this day and are very important! After all, we gain new understanding and innovations because of them.

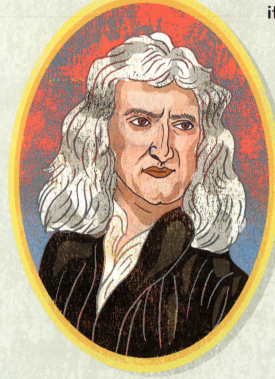

Isaac Newton, 1643-1726

Immanuel Kant, 1724-1804

Time? Absolutely!

Isaac Newton always claimed that he was being copied by everyone. Yet he was a gifted researcher who was interested in an incredible number of subjects. One, for example, was light. He discovered that it is made up of many different wavelengths. He used this theory to build a really good telescope. He observed the stars with it and developed his theory on gravity, for which he is most famous. Newton also maintained that there is an absolute time that passes by at the same speed all over the world. He hoped that there would eventually be clocks accurate enough to prove his theory. Even without proof, people believed he was right for many years, mostly because in our daily lives time does seem to pass quickly, regardless of where you are. Newton would probably be delighted to know that super-accurate atomic clocks exist today. But he would probably be pretty annoyed by the fact that these atomic clocks also prove that his theory on absolute and universally relative time was wrong.

Inner Time

The philosopher, Immanuel Kant, had very different ideas when it came to time. For him, time meant absolutely nothing in terms of what existed outside of ourselves, rather it was a thought device that simply belonged to people. Kant asserted that even though we do not think about time, we would be unable to think without it. For him, the way we see time is some kind of inborn pair of glasses, through which we order the world as past, present, and future. And no matter what, we can't experience our lives without these "glasses."

All Lightning Bolts Are Not Equal

Albert Einstein, 1879-1955

In 1905, Einstein developed his special theory of relativity, in which he stated the one constant in the universe was the speed of light. It moves at 186,000 miles per second. It cannot go any faster.

So Newton said that an hour is an hour for everyone regardless of where they are located. Whether I have an hour to do math in the school up on the mountain or down in the valley, time is the same everywhere. This is what all math teachers thought until the beginning of the twentieth century. And then Albert Einstein (1879-1955) came along. Even as a schoolboy, Einstein pondered the wildest things—phenomena that cannot be observed on earth. How would it be, for example, if you could run side-by-side with the speed of time? Through his tremendous imagination and mathematical ability, he found out that there is no such thing as a constant rate of time.

Relativity of Time

Einstein does not move.
He observes that both lightning bolts flash at the same time.

100 METER

Einstein's friend is moving on the train at great speed.
He sees the lightning bolt in the direction he is moving toward strike first.
Bolt 1: The train and the speed of light are moving toward each other.
Bolt 2: The train is moving away from the lightning bolt. The speed of light takes a fraction longer to catch up to it. That is why bolt 2 comes a bit later for the friend on the train.

100 METER

Both Einstein and his friend are correct in their observations. Based on this theortical experiment, Einstein concludes that time is dependent on the speed at which mass moves. Simultaneity, therefore, is something relative.
Just coming up with such an idea was a stroke of genius. And that was in 1905. But what's going on with the two school classes studying math, one up on the mountain and the other down in the valley? Does one have more time than the other?

On a Spaceship

School time for those on the mountain does actually pass by ever so slightly faster. It is, however, a matter of a millionth of a second, which means you cannot really complain to the teacher.

If the class were to fly through space, however, in some kind of crazy-fast spaceship, then it would be a different story. An hour on the spaceship would pass by slower than on earth. The class on earth would have written at least two hours of math, while those in space would have been traveling for just half an hour.

Crooked Time

Ten years after the special theory of relativity, Einstein discovered that time does some crooked things. Time and space are not only altered by movement and speed, but also by matter. You should imagine space as some type of elastic net and matter as a ball pushing a dent into it, creating a curve in space and time.

1 Just imagine that the sun is a big ball that you place on a trampoline. What happens? It creates a depression. That is exactly how it is with space-time. It bends.

2 When a planet comes close by, it needs to generate enough speed to avoid falling into the depression and not to tumble into the sun. It's the same with earth.

Useful Curvature

The curvature of space-time is part of Einstein's general theory of relativity. Another stroke of genius! Without it there would be no GPS to help us get around. Navigation systems get their information from satellites in space. Given that they orbit about 17,000 miles above earth, the curvature of space-time also needs to be taken into account. Otherwise, our GPS devices would constantly send us on fool's errands.

Powerful Pulling

Newton thought that separate bodies were pulled toward each other. Einstein, on the other hand, asserted that the curvature of space-time (the trampoline) is the cause of this powerful pull. Of course, the trampoline is invisible, but we know today that Einstein was correct. It is due to the curvature of space-time that the little blue ball rotates around the big ball.

A Changing Universe

In the past, the universe was thought to be fixed in place, that all of its planets, stars, and galaxies had always been where they were and would forever stay that way. Einstein was one of the first physicists to suspect that this wasn't the case. His discoveries about the curvature of space-time revealed that all objects in the universe constantly interact with each other, which later led to new ideas about the universe and its beginnings.

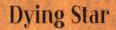

Dying Star

Modern physics has found that two forces act against each other within a star. On the one hand, there is gravity, the force that means a glass of orange juice will fall to the ground if you let go of it. (What a mess!) The individual gravity of stars is a mess, too. It's so strong that stars eventually collapse under their own pressure.

But wait, isn't there energy at the heart of a star that is produced by nuclear fusion? This energy pushes out and acts to counter gravity. For a long time the two forces keep each other in check, like two equally strong giants. Eventually, however, the fuel inside the star burns out. Gravity wins. It pushes inward without resistance and the star disintegrates.

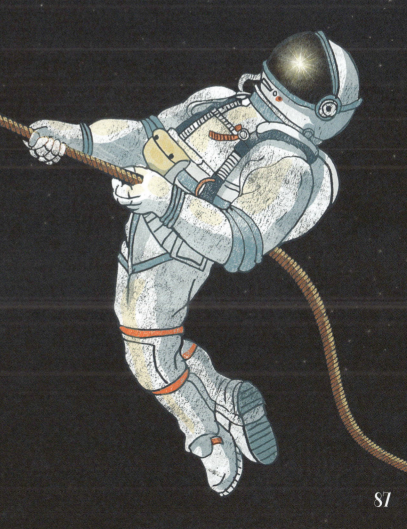

White Dwarf

This has happened to many little stars. It sounds a bit extreme, but from the universe's perspective it does not matter that much. Little stars simply collapse and continue to exist as a shrunken mass. They dead stars are called white dwarfs.

Dead Giant Stars Become ...

There are, however, other, much bigger stars. Real showstoppers. Some have eight times more mass than the sun. But when these giant stars perish, the universe has a problem. What happens is a real game changer because these giant stars become ...

... Black Holes

Dead stars still retain a huge amount of gravitational pull. Everything that isn't far enough away is sucked in and becomes part of the black hole. It's impossible to escape its gravitational field. In 2019, two hundred researchers from around the world were able to capture the first images of a black hole using a virtual giant telescope.

Gravitation vs. Speed

Stars normally don't collide with other planets because they travel so fast. Stars can easily evade the earth's gravitational pull. A speed of 25,057 mph (40,000 kmh) steers them clear of the earth's field of gravity.
To avoid the gravitational field of the sun, a star needs to be a bit faster. 1,242,742 mph (1.9 million kmh) should do the trick. However, there are some collapsed giant stars with such a strong pull that you need to be faster than the speed of light to get away from their gravitational field.
And we know that this is impossible because nothing is faster than the speed of light. Black holes are therefore black because their gravitational pull is so strong that even ultra-fast light cannot escape their pull.

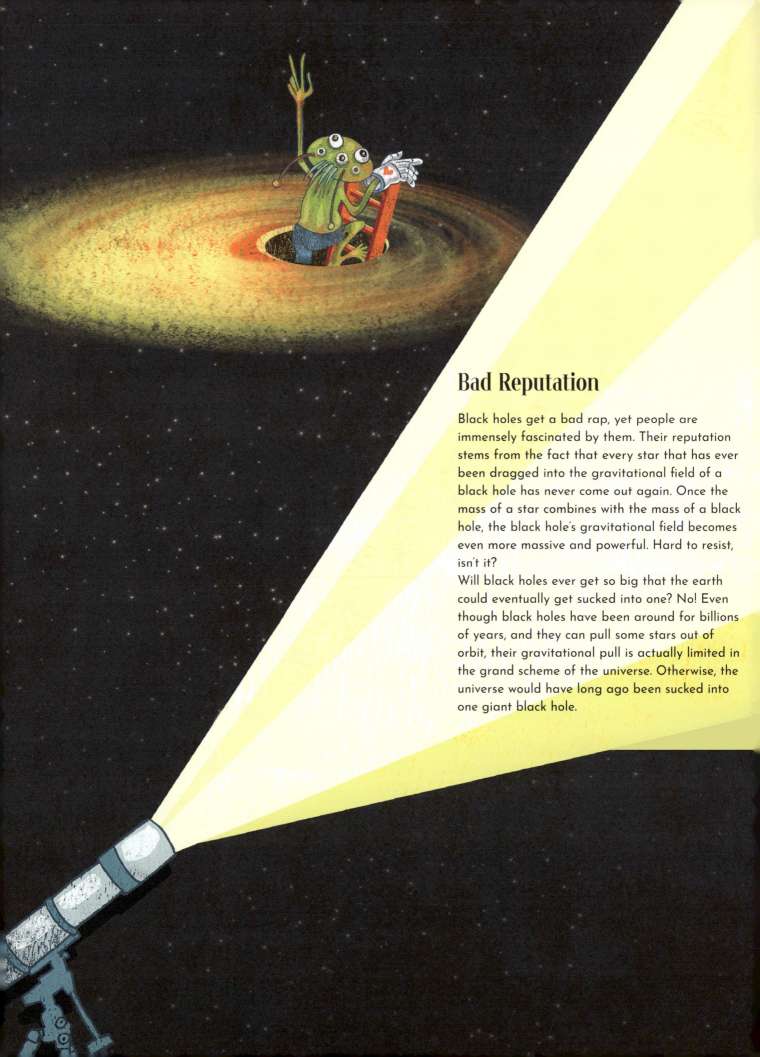

Bad Reputation

Black holes get a bad rap, yet people are immensely fascinated by them. Their reputation stems from the fact that every star that has ever been dragged into the gravitational field of a black hole has never come out again. Once the mass of a star combines with the mass of a black hole, the black hole's gravitational field becomes even more massive and powerful. Hard to resist, isn't it?

Will black holes ever get so big that the earth could eventually get sucked into one? No! Even though black holes have been around for billions of years, and they can pull some stars out of orbit, their gravitational pull is actually limited in the grand scheme of the universe. Otherwise, the universe would have long ago been sucked into one giant black hole.

Wormholes

So why do black holes still fascinate people? Well, it's because we cannot look into them and we do not know where they end. Some people think that black holes could be portals or gateways into other dimensions. A possible door into another time sounds fantastic, doesn't it! But consider the flashing warning signs. First, the nearest black hole in the universe is so far away that you wouldn't be able to reach it in your lifetime. Second, you can't actually travel through a black hole. The immense gravitational forces would tear you apart along the way!

The Big Bang and Time Itself

Black holes prove that the universe is constantly changing. How it looks now is not how it looked in the past. From this we can conclude that the universe must have started at some time or other. Today, our calculations tell us that the universe was created with a big bang around 13.8 billion years ago. But was there a time before that? And how would that have looked?
Physicists today believe that these are the wrong questions to ask. They theorize that the past, present, and future are relative, and in fact, they may never have existed and are just an illusion to make our everyday lives easier. Unfortunately, physical experiments on the big bang cannot be carried out and there are no excavations from that time either, so physics has to rely on imagination and theoretical experiments. But that worked pretty well for Einstein!

Do We Really Want to Go Back to the Future?

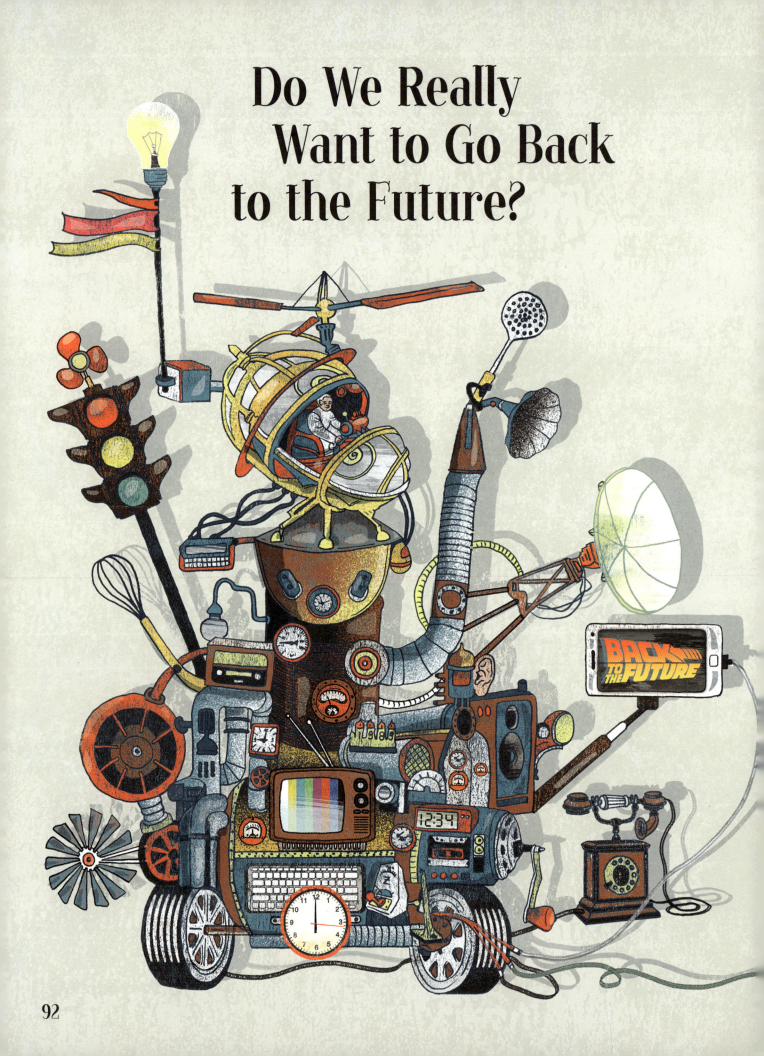

If time is relative, then should we not be able to travel back in time and into the future? Well, the future is one thing and we can look at that later. Traveling to the past, however, does not work according to those who know about physics. There are too many logical problems. Science-fiction writers want to know why. There must have been something to some of Einstein's outlandish notions so why couldn't we try it for once? In this instance, though, physics is absolutely certain. As cool as it would be, traveling back in time is practically impossible.

Science Fiction

Maybe the idea of traveling back in time is so fascinating precisely because physics says it's impossible. There are certainly plenty of stories about it. First, of course, you would need a form of transport to travel back in time.

Time Machines

In the popular movie *Back to the Future*, our time machine is a car! You only need a little bit of plutonium for the nuclear fission in the built-in flux compensator, then with a lot of noise and steam, the car will fly back to the selected year.

It is a bit friendlier on the environment with *Harry Potter and the Prisoner of Azkaban*. Hermione Granger, the studious wizard with far too many classes has a time-turner, which is a small hourglass that she and her fellow travelers simply hang around their necks to travel back in time. However, there are probably not too many of these time-turners about. There are many other time machines you can borrow from stories though: a blue police phone booth, a baby crib, old laptops in a zinc bathtub, and, for those who like to be comfortable, a time-travel sofa.

Time Travel Problems

Even if things are just made up, successful time-travel stories imagine creative solutions to the mind-bending logistics of time travel. What would people in the past think of you? Would they think you were completely crazy and threatening? Would they lock you up in jail so that you were stuck in the wrong time? Or would they think you were a prophet or a fortuneteller? Also, how would traveling to the past change the future? Would you even be alive in the present?

The Butterfly Effect

The meteorologist, Edward N. Lorenz (1917-2008), discovered that even the smallest of changes can have unpredictably major consequences. His famous example theorized that a butterfly flapping its wings in China could affect the weather thousands of miles away a few days later. If the flapping of a butterfly's wings is so significant, then what about time travelers in the past? Even if they've traveled back in time with the best intentions—to correct mistakes or prevent bad events in the future—their presence creates small changes that could lead to all sorts of wildly unforeseeable consequences. And trying to correct the outcomes of their interventions in the past only makes everything worse!

Do Not Mess with the Past!

This is what many time travel stories tell us. Yet that is exactly what ends up happening. So the stories must sort out all the consequences that come from messing with the past, such as finding a different world in the present when the time traveler returns from the past. Because of his or her actions.

Other storytellers maintain that the present only becomes what it is because of the journey into the past. Or they come up with parallel worlds in which each journey to the past creates a different present. The more you travel back in time, the more parallel present realities are created. Welcome to the multiverse! Something Spiderman knows a thing or two about.

The Grandfather Paradox

The grandfather paradox takes the butterfly effect one step further. What if a time traveler kills his grandfather in the past? And before his grandfather met his grandmother? The grandfather and grandmother would not have a child, the mother or father of the time traveler would not exist, and therefore, the time traveler himself would not exist. So here is the paradox: If the time traveler did not exist, how could he travel back in time to kill his grandfather? Maybe time travel is a bit overrated.

Sleeping Beauties, Speeding Spaceships, and Oracles

Now let's get back to the future. Traveling *forward* in time can't be as bad going backward, can it? Especially since there about half as many logistical issues to face.

Sleeping Beauty

Actually, we are on a journey into the future
all the time. Let's say we are Sleeping Beauty
and we sleep for ten years. When we wake up,
we definitely feel as if we have been traveling
through time. Surely, lots must have happened
while we were snoring away. There are just two
small problems here. We would not come back if
we only want to hear about the past ten years.
Because that would be a journey into the past.
And besides, it's all a fairytale trick. Freezing your
consciousness for ten years and then waking up
is such a ruse. It could only happen in fairy tales.

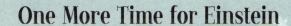

One More Time for Einstein

Maybe we'll forget about the Sleeping Beauty technique. Albert Einstein
might have had a better method.
All you need is a spaceship and a space traveler (you). Jump in. Shut the
door. Countdown to blast off. Then let's zoom through space and time.
Maybe you are in the universe for about three months. Time goes by quite
normally for you. After three months you've had enough of all that space, so
you return to earth, where only a year or two would have passed since you
left. It all depends on how fast your spaceship flew. The faster you zoom,
the more time passes on earth, which means you would have traveled to
the future.
There is, though, a minor problem here as well. We do not yet have space-
ships that are that fast. But we've proven Einstein's theory in an experiment
using two atomic clocks. One stayed on earth and one flew in a superfast
plane. After landing, it was discovered that time onboard the airplane had
actually gone by a little more slowly than the on earth!

The Future Is Now

Enough of these imaginary journeys to the future. Do we really want to be out in space while our loved ones get old on earth? Humans have always dreamed about getting a sneak preview of their own future. Truth is, if you look around, you might see signs of it already in the present!

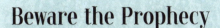

Beware the Prophecy

People have been trying for as long as we can remember to peer into the future. The ancient Greeks, for example, regularly consulted oracles—priests or priestesses who received direct messages from the gods about the future. We also try to see the future by reading the stars, tea leaves, coffee grounds, playing cards, and crystal balls. But do we really want to know the future? What do we hope to accomplish with that knowledge? Are you trying to change the future? Does the past not matter? Our science fictions and fairy tales are often about characters desperately trying to escape their fates. Remember what happened to old Kronos. Maybe he shouldn't have listened to the prediction that his children would snatch power from him. He might have been better off if he'd just been nicer to them in the first place.

The Future in the Past

It is much more exciting, however, to look at the way people used to imagine the future that we live in today. The filmmakers of *Back to the Future II*, for example, imagined that young people would have flying skateboards by now. A cool idea, but sadly it has yet to happen. On the other hand, nowadays everyone has an even better version of a *Star Trek* communicator. And less than fifty years ago everyday video communications seemed like a wild fantasy from the distant future, but it's also a reality we all—well, maybe not our grandparents—take for granted.

However, there is a way of getting in touch with your own future.

Letter to My Future Self

Hi you! Sorry, I mean me. If you, I mean I, are reading this letter, then you are 10 years older than I am now, or you were then? I can't even imagine it—you, me—us—ten years from now. That's why I'll write you what's important to me now. Maybe you'll find that a bit silly then. But I'll write it anyway just so you don't forget. Here we go …

Index

© 2020, Prestel Verlag, Munich · London · New York
A member of Verlagsgruppe Random House GmbH
Neumarkter Strasse 28 · 81673 Munich
© Texts: 2020, Kathrin Köller
© Illustrations: 2020, Irmela Schautz

Prestel Publishing Ltd.
14-17 Wells Street
London W1T 3PD

Prestel Publishing
900 Broadway, Suite 603
New York, NY 10003

Library of Congress Control Number:
2019949135
A CIP catalogue record for this book is available
from the British Library.

Translated from German by Paul Kelly
Editorial direction: Doris Kutschbach
Project management: Melanie Schöni
Copyediting: John Son
Design and layout: Meike Sellier
Production management: Susanne Hermann
Printing and binding: DZS Grafik d.o.o.
Paper: Tauro Offset

MIX
Paper from
responsible sources
FSC® C106600

Verlagsgruppe Random House FSC® N001967

Printed in Slovenia

ISBN 978-3-7913-7417-8
www.prestel.com